CHUCK

GROW

JOURNAL

crossroads

Copyright © 2022 by Crossroads Christian Church
CrossroadsChurch.com | @CrossroadsCA

All rights reserved.

Independently published.
ISBN: 9798357322319

Scripture taken from The NEW AMERICAN STANDARD BIBLE®, Copyright © 1960, 1962, 1963 1968, 1971, 1972, 1973 1975, 1977, 1995, 2022 by The Lockman Foundation. Used by permission. www.lockman.org

Scripture quotations marked (NLT) are taken from The Holy Bible, New Living Translation, Copyright © 1996, 2004, 2015 by Tyndale House Foundation. Used by permission of Tyndale House Publishers, Carol Stream, Illinois 60188 www.tyndale.com

Scripture quotations marked (ESV®) are taken from The Holy Bible, English Standard Version® (ESV®), Copyright © 2001 by Crossway, a publishing ministry of Good News Publishers. Used by permission of Crossway / Good News Publishers, Wheaton, Illinois 60187
www.crossway.org

(PSALM 1:3)

GROW Deep Roots

He will be like a tree firmly planted by streams of water, which yields its fruit in its season & its leaf does not wither; and in whatever he does, he prospers.

Contents

05. MY COMMITMENT TO GROW

06. THE VISION OF THE TREE OF LIFE

07. WHAT DOES IT MEAN TO BE A DISCIPLE OF JESUS?

08. THE WAY WE BECOME DISCIPLES

09. THE WAY OF DISCIPLESHIP

10. HOW TO USE THIS JOURNAL

12. **WEEK 1:** Last Days Update

33. **WEEK 2:** G: Get in the Word | R: Receive Instruction

58. **WEEK 3:** O: Obey from the Heart: Time & Talent

86. **WEEK 4:** O: Obey from the Heart: Treasure & Testimony

112. **WEEK 5:** W: Worship with Passion

134. **WEEK 6:** Identity and Purpose

144. CONCLUSION

MY COMMITMENT TO
GROW

Get in God's Word.
☐ I will meet with the Lord every day for the next three years asking Him to teach me as I read His Word.

Receive Instruction.
☐ I will be in a place of in-depth study where I receive instruction from God's Word at least one time a week along with being a part of the Weekend service either in person or online.

Obey from the Heart.
☐ Time: I will see my time as something I commit to God by spending time with Him, investing in every First Wednesday and spending time serving Him.

☐ Talent: I will discover my Spiritual Gift. I will then seek to find a place to serve God in the Church using my gift.

☐ Treasure: I will be faithful with the financial resources God has blessed me with.
  ☐ I will give God a full tithe of the first ten percent of all income I receive.
  My tithe amount is: $_____
  ☐ I will give offerings to God as He blesses me.
  This year, I will give God an offering of

  $_____ as He blesses me.

☐ Testimony: I will share my testimony of what God is doing in my life with people who I know are far from God and His love.

Worship with Passion
☐ I will commit to passionately worshiping God at our First Wednesday services either in person or online for the next three years.

Signed: **Date:**

> Our vision at Crossroads is to be a tree of life with roots that go deeper and a trunk that gets stronger. Then the tree will flourish, yielding broad branches and bearing fruit.

THE VISION OF THE
Tree of Life

This vision is for our church and each individual who is a part of the Crossroads family. We want to have a deep-rooted faith that goes ever deeper. We want to have a strong and increasing faith that grows ever stronger. When this becomes your reality then you will be the disciple that Jesus has called you to be. You will have a deep faith in Him and a growing faith in Him. You grow ever closer to Him.

Jesus said when we have faith like a mustard seed then we will see mulberry trees uprooted and mountains will move. We will see miracles take place and experience the power of God *(Luke 17:6 & Matthew 17:20)*. This vision will take you to a place where you deepen and grow your faith so that you will see miracles happen. This is how we go from saying we believe to really believing. This is how we go from talking about being a Christian to living by the power of God. This is how we become true disciples of Jesus Christ.

1 CORINTHIANS 4:20 (NLT)
²⁰ For the Kingdom of God is not just a lot of talk; it is living by God's power.

This is how we live a life of faith where we see the blessings of God become miraculous.

ISAIAH 41:19-20 (NLT)
¹⁹ I will plant trees in the barren desert— cedar, acacia, myrtle, olive, cypress, fir, and pine.
²⁰ I am doing this so all who see this miracle will understand what it means— that it is the Lord who has done this, the Holy One of Israel who created it.

WHAT DOES IT MEAN TO BE A DISCIPLE OF JESUS?

Jesus defined what a Disciple is in Matthew 10:24-25 and in John 13:33-34.

MATTHEW 10:24-25A (NASB)
²⁴ "A disciple is not above his teacher, nor a slave above his master.
²⁵ "It is enough for the disciple that he become like his teacher, and the slave like his master.

JOHN 13:34-35 (NASB)
³⁴ "A new commandment I give to you, that you love one another, even as I have loved you, that you also love one another.
³⁵ "By this all men will know that you are My disciples, if you have love for one another."

In these two passages we see that there are 3 "L's" of Discipleship
1. **Lordship:** where Jesus is lord of our lives.
2. **Likeness:** where we become more and more like Jesus.
3. **Love:** where we love other Christians like family.

As we seek to GROW in discipleship then each of these "L's" will become true of us. This means we will be disciples of Jesus in reality and have a faith that is so real it goes deeper and grows stronger.

Jesus took 3 years to GROW His followers into disciples. I believe you and I need to commit to 3 years of living out GROW so we will become true disciples of Jesus.

I also know this is the best life you can and will ever live. Paul tells us this is what the Bible's message is.

1 CORINTHIANS 2:9-10 (NLT)
> **9** That is what the Scriptures mean when they say, "No eye has seen, no ear has heard, and no mind has imagined what God has prepared for those who love Him."
> **10** But it was to us that God revealed these things by His Spirit. For His Spirit searches out everything and shows us God's deep secrets.

THE WAY WE BECOME DISCIPLES

Jesus gave us the great commission which is to go into all the world and make disciples from every ethnic group. In that commission we see the way disciples are made.

MATTHEW 28:18-20 (NASB)
> **18** And Jesus came up and spoke to them, saying, "All authority has been given to Me in heaven and on earth.
> **19** "Go therefore and make disciples of all the nations, baptizing them in the name of the Father and the Son and the Holy Spirit,
> **20** teaching them to observe all that I commanded you; and lo, I am with you always, even to the end of the age."

THE WAY OF DISCIPLESHIP IS...

- We are to be baptized (by full immersion) in the name of the Father, the Son and the Holy Spirit. When we are baptized by full immersion we are being buried with Christ (Romans 6) in a worship experience where we are committing completely to living our lives with Christ and for Christ.
  - Have you been baptized?
- We are taught to observe all that Jesus commands us. This is why the first two letters of GROW are so important to us being Disciples. We need to *Get in God's Word everyday*. We need to *Receive Instruction* so we can be taught all Jesus commands us.
  - Are you ready to commit to receiving instruction outside of the Sunday gathering for the next three years?

The call for us to follow Jesus and be His disciples is a call to a life beyond imagination. One that is real. One that brings us back to the Tree of Life and takes us in the way of miracles.

So let's commit to GROW.

In Christ,

Chuck Booher

HOW TO Use This Journal

This Journal is broken up into 6 weeks and each week has 3 sections. The best way to do this journal is to:

1. **Read and prep before Sunday's message** — Read and answer the questions I wrote to prepare for the Sunday message.
2. **Hear the message and take notes** — Join us every Sunday in-person or online as we GROW together! Use the sermon notes page to take notes.
3. **Study and dig deeper on your own** — For the next seven days after the Sunday message, use the SOAP method to study and dig deeper the principles we discussed in the Sunday message.

SOAP method of Bible Study

One method of Bible study that people use to get into the word of God and get the word into them is the SOAP method of Bible study. SOAP is an acrostic that will guide you in digging deeper into the word of God.

You start your time with God by praying. You ask God to draw you close (James 4:8) and ask Him to teach you and guide you as you read His word. Then you open your Bible to the section of scripture you are studying and you read the word. As you read, you look for a passage of scripture to stand out to you in a special way. Then you go through the SOAP method.

S: Scripture.
- Write down the Scripture.
- Read the passage that God is bringing to mind in a couple of different translations.

O: Observations.
Pray and ask God to show you things in the passage and in your key verse. Write down:
- Who is being talked to.
- What is being said to them.
    - What commands are found in this passage?
    - What warnings are given?
    - What promises are made?
- Where is this being said or written from and is that important to what you are reading?
- Are there words that are emphasized and/or being used more than once?
- What are the definitions of important words?
- Using a tool for cross-referencing, what do other verses in the Bible add to your understanding of this verse or passage?
- Looking at commentaries or Study Bible notes, what do you learn about this passage?
- How does what you learn help you understand and know God better?

A: Application.
- What does this mean to you?
- How does this apply to your life?
- Is there a command you should obey?
- Is there something you should start or stop doing?
- Is there a promise you should claim as a believer in Christ?

P: Prayer.
- Write out or pray based on what you have learned and what the Lord wants to apply to your life.
- Ask God to move in your heart and fill you with His Spirit as you pray this.
- Pray for others that God is bringing to mind as you were studying this section of scripture.

WEEK 1:
Last Days Update

We are living in the most exciting time in all of history. We are very close to the Second Coming of Jesus Christ.

When Jesus came the first time those who studied the prophecies of the Old Testament knew He was coming and they knew the time and place of His coming.

Today we can see the signs of His second coming. What we need to be aware of is that God deliberately created us to fulfill an amazing purpose in these last days.

We also need to be sure that we are ready for when Jesus comes. This means we need to be serious about being His disciples in these last days.

For more information on the reason why we know we are in the Last Days, see this message from May 2021: *What Biblical Prophecies Have Been Fulfilled* at **www.CrossroadsChurch.com/growjournal**

READ MATTHEW 16:2-3 (NLT)
> [2] He replied, "You know the saying, 'Red sky at night means fair weather tomorrow; [3] red sky in the morning means foul weather all day.' You know how to interpret the weather signs in the sky, but you don't know how to interpret the signs of the times!

Jesus is telling the Pharisees that they aren't paying attention to what is happening in their current times.

Do you feel like you know how to read the signs of our times?

READ 1 THESSALONIANS 5:1-8 (NASB)

¹ Now as to the times and the epochs, brethren, you have no need of anything to be written to you. ² For you yourselves know full well that the day of the Lord will come just like a thief in the night. ³ While they are saying, "Peace and safety!" Then destruction will come upon them suddenly like labor pains upon a woman with child, and they will not escape.

⁴ But you, brethren, are not in darkness, that the day would overtake you like a thief; ⁵ for you are all sons of light and sons of day. We are not of night nor of darkness; ⁶ so then let us not sleep as others do, but let us be alert and sober. ⁷ For those who sleep do their sleeping at night, and those who get drunk get drunk at night. ⁸ But since we are of the day, let us be sober, having put on the breastplate of faith and love, and as a helmet, the hope of salvation.

What does Paul tell us Jesus' Second Coming will be like? Who are the ones who are saying peace and safety? What does Paul say should be true of believers and their knowledge of the coming of the Lord? How does Paul say we should live knowing the times we are living in?

READ LUKE 21:25-36 (NASB)

²⁵ "There will be signs in sun and moon and stars, and on the earth dismay among nations, in perplexity at the roaring of the sea and the

waves, **26** men fainting from fear and the expectation of the things which are coming upon the world; for the powers of the heavens will be shaken. **27** "Then they will see the Son of Man coming in a cloud with power and great glory. **28** "But when these things begin to take place, straighten up and lift up your heads, because your redemption is drawing near."

29 Then He told them a parable: "Behold the fig tree and all the trees; **30** as soon as they put forth leaves, you see it and know for yourselves that summer is now near. **31** "So you also, when you see these things happening, recognize that the kingdom of God is near. **32** "Truly I say to you, this generation will not pass away until all things take place. **33** "Heaven and earth will pass away, but My words will not pass away.

34 "Be on guard, so that your hearts will not be weighted down with dissipation and drunkenness and the worries of life, and that day will not come on you suddenly like a trap; **35** for it will come upon all those who dwell on the face of all the earth. **36** "But keep on the alert at all times, praying that you may have strength to escape all these things that are about to take place, and to stand before the Son of Man."

What does Jesus say are some signs we will see happen just before He comes again? When we see these signs taking place, what are we told to do?

_____

_____

What does the fig tree teach us in regards to Jesus' coming? When these things start to take place, what does Jesus say we should do?

_____

_____

What are we to be on guard from? Do you feel you are ready for the coming of the Lord?

_____

_____

DATE
October 30th

SERMON TITLE

SPEAKER

Sermon notes

Hear the message and take notes

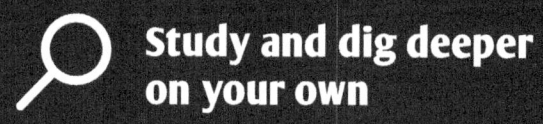

Study and dig deeper on your own

Use the SOAP method to review these scriptures we studied in the Last Days Update section

DAY 1

S: Scripture. READ MATTHEW 16:2-3 (NLT)
² He replied, "You know the saying, 'Red sky at night means fair weather tomorrow; ³ red sky in the morning means foul weather all day.' You know how to interpret the weather signs in the sky, but you don't know how to interpret the signs of the times!

O: Observations. Pray and ask God to show you things in the passage and in your key verse.
Who is being talked to?

___

What is being said to them? (What commands are found in this passage? What warnings are given? What promises are made?)

___

Where is this being said or written from and is that important to what you are reading?

___

Are there words that are emphasized and/or being used more than once? What are the definitions of important words?

___

Using a tool for cross-referencing, what do other verses in the Bible add to your understanding of this verse or passage?

___

Looking at commentaries or Study Bible notes, what do you learn about this passage?

_____
_____
_____

How does what you learn help you understand and know God better?

_____
_____
_____

A: Application. What does this mean to you? How does this apply to your life?

_____
_____

Is there a command you should obey? Is there something you should start or stop doing? Is there a promise you should claim as a believer in Christ?

_____
_____

P: Prayer. Write out or pray based on what you have learned and what the Lord wants to apply to your life. Ask God to move in your heart and fill you with His Spirit as you pray this. Pray for others that God is bringing to mind as you were studying this section of scripture.

_____
_____
_____
_____
_____

DAY 2

S: Scripture. 1 THESSALONIANS 5:1-8 (NASB)

¹ Now as to the times and the epochs, brethren, you have no need of anything to be written to you. ² For you yourselves know full well that the day of the Lord will come just like a thief in the night. ³ While they are saying, "Peace and safety!" Then destruction will come upon them suddenly like labor pains upon a woman with child, and they will not escape.

⁴ But you, brethren, are not in darkness, that the day would overtake you like a thief; ⁵ for you are all sons of light and sons of day. We are not of night nor of darkness; ⁶ so then let us not sleep as others do, but let us be alert and sober. ⁷ For those who sleep do their sleeping at night, and those who get drunk get drunk at night. ⁸ But since we are of the day, let us be sober, having put on the breastplate of faith and love, and as a helmet, the hope of salvation.

O: Observations. Pray and ask God to show you things in the passage and in your key verse.

Who is being talked to?

_____

What is being said to them? (What commands are found in this passage? What warnings are given? What promises are made?)

_____

_____

Where is this being said or written from and is that important to what you are reading?

_____

_____

Are there words that are emphasized and/or being used more than once? What are the definitions of important words?

_____

_____

Using a tool for cross-referencing, what do other verses in the Bible add to your understanding of this verse or passage?

Looking at commentaries or Study Bible notes, what do you learn about this passage?

How does what you learn help you understand and know God better?

A: Application. What does this mean to you? How does this apply to your life?

Is there a command you should obey? Is there something you should start or stop doing? Is there a promise you should claim as a believer in Christ?

P: Prayer. Write out or pray based on what you have learned and what the Lord wants to apply to your life. Ask God to move in your heart and fill you with His Spirit as you pray this. Pray for others that God is bringing to mind as you were studying this section of scripture.

DAY 3

S: Scripture. READ LUKE 21:25-28 (NASB)

²⁵ "There will be signs in sun and moon and stars, and on the earth dismay among nations, in perplexity at the roaring of the sea and the waves,
²⁶ men fainting from fear and the expectation of the things which are coming upon the world; for the powers of the heavens will be shaken.
²⁷ "Then they will see the Son of Man coming in a cloud with power and great glory. ²⁸ "But when these things begin to take place, straighten up and lift up your heads, because your redemption is drawing near."

O: Observations. Pray and ask God to show you things in the passage and in your key verse.

Who is being talked to?

_____

What is being said to them? (What commands are found in this passage? What warnings are given? What promises are made?)

_____

Where is this being said or written from and is that important to what you are reading?

_____

Are there words that are emphasized and/or being used more than once? What are the definitions of important words?

_____

Using a tool for cross-referencing, what do other verses in the Bible add to your understanding of this verse or passage?

_____

Looking at commentaries or Study Bible notes, what do you learn about this passage?

_____
_____
_____

How does what you learn help you understand and know God better?

_____
_____
_____

A: Application. What does this mean to you? How does this apply to your life?

_____
_____

Is there a command you should obey? Is there something you should start or stop doing? Is there a promise you should claim as a believer in Christ?

_____
_____

P: Prayer. Write out or pray based on what you have learned and what the Lord wants to apply to your life. Ask God to move in your heart and fill you with His Spirit as you pray this. Pray for others that God is bringing to mind as you were studying this section of scripture.

_____
_____
_____
_____
_____

DAY 4

S: Scripture. READ LUKE 21:29-33 (NASB)

²⁹ Then He told them a parable: "Behold the fig tree and all the trees; ³⁰ as soon as they put forth leaves, you see it and know for yourselves that summer is now near. ³¹ "So you also, when you see these things happening, recognize that the kingdom of God is near. ³² "Truly I say to you, this generation will not pass away until all things take place.
³³ "Heaven and earth will pass away, but My words will not pass away.

O: Observations. Pray and ask God to show you things in the passage and in your key verse.

Who is being talked to?

_____

What is being said to them? (What commands are found in this passage? What warnings are given? What promises are made?)

_____

Where is this being said or written from and is that important to what you are reading?

_____

Are there words that are emphasized and/or being used more than once? What are the definitions of important words?

_____

Using a tool for cross-referencing, what do other verses in the Bible add to your understanding of this verse or passage?

_____

Looking at commentaries or Study Bible notes, what do you learn about this passage?

_____
_____
_____

How does what you learn help you understand and know God better?

_____
_____
_____
_____

A: Application. What does this mean to you? How does this apply to your life?

_____
_____

Is there a command you should obey? Is there something you should start or stop doing? Is there a promise you should claim as a believer in Christ?

_____
_____

P: Prayer. Write out or pray based on what you have learned and what the Lord wants to apply to your life. Ask God to move in your heart and fill you with His Spirit as you pray this. Pray for others that God is bringing to mind as you were studying this section of scripture.

_____
_____
_____
_____
_____

DAY 5

S: Scripture. READ LUKE 21:34-36 (NASB)

³⁴ "Be on guard, so that your hearts will not be weighted down with dissipation and drunkenness and the worries of life, and that day will not come on you suddenly like a trap; ³⁵ for it will come upon all those who dwell on the face of all the earth. ³⁶ "But keep on the alert at all times, praying that you may have strength to escape all these things that are about to take place, and to stand before the Son of Man."

O: Observations. Pray and ask God to show you things in the passage and in your key verse.

Who is being talked to?

What is being said to them? (What commands are found in this passage? What warnings are given? What promises are made?)

Where is this being said or written from and is that important to what you are reading?

Are there words that are emphasized and/or being used more than once? What are the definitions of important words?

Using a tool for cross-referencing, what do other verses in the Bible add to your understanding of this verse or passage?

Looking at commentaries or Study Bible notes, what do you learn about this passage?

_____
_____
_____

How does what you learn help you understand and know God better?

_____
_____
_____

A: Application. What does this mean to you? How does this apply to your life?

_____
_____

Is there a command you should obey? Is there something you should start or stop doing? Is there a promise you should claim as a believer in Christ?

_____
_____

P: Prayer. Write out or pray based on what you have learned and what the Lord wants to apply to your life. Ask God to move in your heart and fill you with His Spirit as you pray this. Pray for others that God is bringing to mind as you were studying this section of scripture.

_____
_____
_____
_____
_____

DAY 6

S: Scripture. MATTHEW 28:18-20 (NASB)

¹⁸ And Jesus came up and spoke to them, saying, "All authority has been given to Me in heaven and on earth.
¹⁹ "Go therefore and make disciples of all the nations, baptizing them in the name of the Father and the Son and the Holy Spirit,
²⁰ teaching them to observe all that I commanded you; and lo, I am with you always, even to the end of the age."

O: Observations. Pray and ask God to show you things in the passage and in your key verse.

Who is being talked to?

What is being said to them? (What commands are found in this passage? What warnings are given? What promises are made?)

Where is this being said or written from and is that important to what you are reading?

Are there words that are emphasized and/or being used more than once? What are the definitions of important words?

Using a tool for cross-referencing, what do other verses in the Bible add to your understanding of this verse or passage?

Looking at commentaries or Study Bible notes, what do you learn about this passage?

_____
_____
_____

How does what you learn help you understand and know God better?

_____
_____
_____

A: Application. What does this mean to you? How does this apply to your life?

_____
_____
_____

Is there a command you should obey? Is there something you should start or stop doing? Is there a promise you should claim as a believer in Christ?

_____
_____

P: Prayer. Write out or pray based on what you have learned and what the Lord wants to apply to your life. Ask God to move in your heart and fill you with His Spirit as you pray this. Pray for others that God is bringing to mind as you were studying this section of scripture.

_____
_____
_____
_____
_____

DAY 7

S: Scripture. JOHN 13:34-35 (NASB)
34 "A new commandment I give to you, that you love one another, even as I have loved you, that you also love one another.
35 "By this all men will know that you are My disciples, if you have love for one another."

O: Observations. Pray and ask God to show you things in the passage and in your key verse.

Who is being talked to?

What is being said to them? (What commands are found in this passage? What warnings are given? What promises are made?)

Where is this being said or written from and is that important to what you are reading?

Are there words that are emphasized and/or being used more than once? What are the definitions of important words?

Using a tool for cross-referencing, what do other verses in the Bible add to your understanding of this verse or passage?

Looking at commentaries or Study Bible notes, what do you learn about this passage?

_____
_____
_____

How does what you learn help you understand and know God better?

_____
_____
_____

A: Application. What does this mean to you? How does this apply to your life?

_____
_____

Is there a command you should obey? Is there something you should start or stop doing? Is there a promise you should claim as a believer in Christ?

_____
_____

P: Prayer. Write out or pray based on what you have learned and what the Lord wants to apply to your life. Ask God to move in your heart and fill you with His Spirit as you pray this. Pray for others that God is bringing to mind as you were studying this section of scripture.

_____
_____
_____
_____
_____

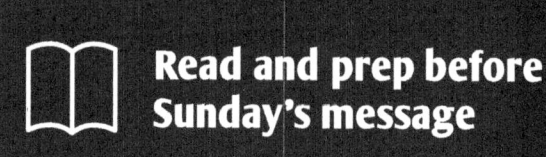
Read and prep before Sunday's message

WEEK 2
G: Get in God's Word

Jesus said that "if" we continue in His word then we are truly His disciples. "If" means we have a choice and I am hoping you will choose to get in His word and even more, to get His word into you.

The Reveal Study was conducted on people who attend Church and the main finding was that nothing brought true transformation than being in God's Word every day. So, as we all commit together to get in God's Word, then get ready for the Spirit of God to bring true change and transformation in you and in your life.

READ JOHN 8:31-32 (NASB)
> 31 So Jesus was saying to those Jews who had believed Him, "If you continue in My word, then you are truly disciples of Mine;
> 32 and you will know the truth, and the truth will make you free."

What does Jesus call for us to do? What will this make us if we do this?

_____

_____

What is the result Jesus promises will occur if we do this? What is it that you believe Jesus will free you from?

_____

_____

READ PSALM 1:1-3 (NASB)

¹ How blessed is the man who does not walk in the counsel of the wicked,
Nor stand in the path of sinners,
Nor sit in the seat of scoffers!
² But his delight is in the law of the Lord,
And in His law he meditates day and night.
³ He will be like a tree firmly planted by streams of water,
Which yields its fruit in its season And its leaf does not wither;
And in whatever he does, he prospers.

What do you think being blessed means?
What does a blessed person do and not do?

_____
_____
_____
_____

What are the results if you are actively studying and meditating on the word of God every day? The promise is given with imagery that you need to apply to your life; what practically will occur if you are a person who delights in the Law of the Lord and meditates on His word?

_____
_____
_____
_____

READ JOSHUA 1:7-8 (NASB)

⁷ "Only be strong and very courageous; be careful to do according to all the law which Moses My servant commanded you; do not turn from it to the right or to the left, so that you may have success wherever you go.
⁸ "This book of the law shall not depart from your mouth, but you shall meditate on it day and night, so that you may be careful to do according to all that is written in it; for then you will make your way prosperous, and then you will have success.

Joshua is now assuming the role of leading the Children of Israel from Moses. What does God tell him he is to do? How does this align with what all of us are told to do and what will happen in Psalm 1:1-3?

How do you see success and prosperity happening in your life if you are in the word of God daily? Do you believe that you can trust God to fulfill these promises?

SUGGESTED
Bible Reading Plan

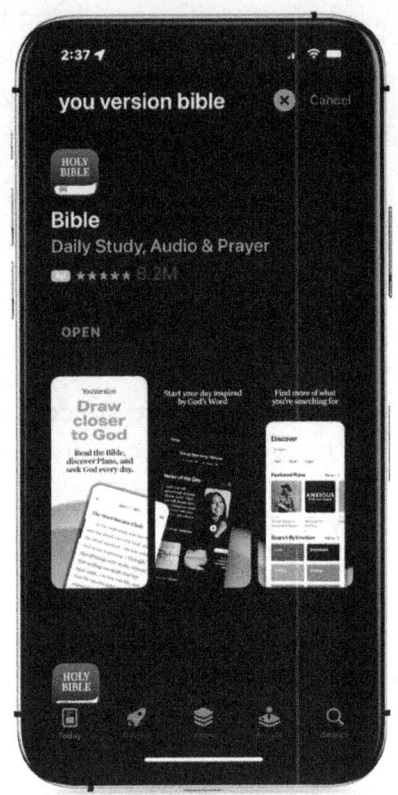

One way to be consistent with *Getting into the Word* is using a Bible Reading Plan. We have suggested a plan where you will read through the Bible chronologically in one year.

The suggested way to do this is on the **YouVersion Bible** App, which is free. This App will keep track of the days you read and allow you to read in multiple versions of the Bible. It also will allow you to listen to the Bible on audio so you can do this while you drive.

To get the app and to interact with others from Crossroads who are reading the same scriptures each day, **scan the QR code and select Crossroads** as your church or go to www.CrossroadsChurch.com/growjournal!

WEEK 2
R: Receive Instruction

For each of us to come to faith and grow deeper in our faith, we need to be taught the word of God. Jesus spent three years teaching His followers His word. You and I need to commit to be learners for our whole lives. If we do then we will always be growing in our faith and going deeper in our relationship with Him.

READ ROMANS 10:17 (NASB)

¹⁷ So faith *comes* from hearing, and hearing by the word of Christ.

How does faith come to us? What does it mean to hear by the word of Christ?

_____

_____

READ GALATIANS 3:2-5 (NASB)

² This is the only thing I want to find out from you: did you receive the Spirit by the works of the Law, or by hearing with faith? ³ Are you so foolish? Having begun by the Spirit, are you now being perfected by the flesh? ⁴ Did you suffer so many things in vain—if indeed it was in vain? ⁵ So then, does He who provides you with the Spirit and works miracles among you, do it by the works of the Law, or by hearing with faith?

The apostle Paul is asking these questions to the Galation church to make a point to them: we are saved by faith and not by the law.

What are the results of the hearing of faith? Are you seeing these results in your life? If you dedicate yourself to being in a place where you are taught the word of God and hear the teaching in faith, will this happen for you?

_____
_____
_____

READ EPHESIANS 4:11-13 (NASB)
> 11 And He gave some as apostles, and some as prophets, and some as evangelists, and some as pastors and teachers, 12 for the equipping of the saints for the work of service, to the building up of the body of Christ; 13 until we all attain to the unity of the faith, and of the knowledge of the Son of God, to a mature man, to the measure of the stature which belongs to the fullness of Christ.

What kinds of leaders did God give to the Church and to you as a believer?

_____

What is the purpose of each of these people using their gifts? How does this make you stronger and better in your faith?

_____
_____

These two passages warn what happens when there is no one teaching and no one receiving instruction.

READ 2 CHRONICLES 15:1-3 (NASB)
> 1 Now the Spirit of God came on Azariah the son of Oded, 2 and he went out to meet Asa and said to him, "Listen to me, Asa, and all Judah and Benjamin: the Lord is with you when you are with Him. And if you seek Him, He will let you find Him; but if you forsake Him, He will forsake you. 3 "For many days Israel was without the true God and without a teaching priest and without law.

READ AMOS 8:11-13 (NASB)

> ¹¹ "Behold, days are coming," declares the Lord God, "When I will send a famine on the land, not a famine for bread or a thirst for water, but rather for hearing the words of the Lord. ¹² "People will stagger from sea to sea and from the north even to the east; They will go to and fro to seek the word of the Lord, but they will not find it. ¹³ "In that day the beautiful virgins and the young men will faint from thirst.

What does God promise King Asa and all of us? What was the consequence for this not being true of Israel?

_____

_____

What are people not getting that they all desperately need? What are the results of not being able to hear or be taught the word of the Lord? Are you seeing this occur today?

_____

_____

_____

We have two main ways for you to get into a place to receive instruction. One is our Wednesday night service. This is a service where the teaching will be deeper so that you can have deeper roots and a stronger trunk.

The other place where you can receive instruction is by doing a study (on your own or with a group) through our House of Study at **www.CrossroadsChurch.com/growjournal**

Hear the message and take notes

Sermon notes

DATE
November 6th

SERMON TITLE

SPEAKER

Study and dig deeper on your own

Use the SOAP method to review the scriptures we studied in the Get in God's Word and Receive Instruction sections

DAY 1

S: Scripture. READ JOHN 8:31–32 (NASB)

³¹ So Jesus was saying to those Jews who had believed Him, "If you continue in My word, then you are truly disciples of Mine;
³² and you will know the truth, and the truth will make you free."

O: Observations. Pray and ask God to show you things in the passage and in your key verse.

Who is being talked to?

_____
_____

What is being said to them? (What commands are found in this passage? What warnings are given? What promises are made?)

_____
_____

Where is this being said or written from and is that important to what you are reading?

_____
_____

Are there words that are emphasized and/or being used more than once? What are the definitions of important words?

_____
_____

Using a tool for cross-referencing, what do other verses in the Bible add to your understanding of this verse or passage?

_____
_____

Looking at commentaries or Study Bible notes, what do you learn about this passage?

How does what you learn help you understand and know God better?

A: Application. What does this mean to you? How does this apply to your life?

Is there a command you should obey? Is there something you should start or stop doing? Is there a promise you should claim as a believer in Christ?

P: Prayer. Write out or pray based on what you have learned and what the Lord wants to apply to your life. Ask God to move in your heart and fill you with His Spirit as you pray this. Pray for others that God is bringing to mind as you were studying this section of scripture.

DAY 2

S: Scripture. READ PSALM 1:1-3 (NASB)
¹ How blessed is the man who does not walk in the
counsel of the wicked,
Nor stand in the path of sinners,
Nor sit in the seat of scoffers!
² But his delight is in the law of the Lord,
And in His law he meditates day and night.
³ He will be like a tree firmly planted by streams of water, Which yields its fruit in its season And its leaf does not wither; And in whatever he does, he prospers.

O: Observations. Pray and ask God to show you things in the passage and in your key verse.
Who is being talked to?

_____

What is being said to them? (What commands are found in this passage? What warnings are given? What promises are made?)

_____

_____

Where is this being said or written from and is that important to what you are reading?

_____

_____

Are there words that are emphasized and/or being used more than once? What are the definitions of important words?

_____

_____

Using a tool for cross-referencing, what do other verses in the Bible add to your understanding of this verse or passage?

_____

_____

Looking at commentaries or Study Bible notes, what do you learn about this passage?

How does what you learn help you understand and know God better?

A: Application. What does this mean to you? How does this apply to your life?

Is there a command you should obey? Is there something you should start or stop doing? Is there a promise you should claim as a believer in Christ?

P: Prayer. Write out or pray based on what you have learned and what the Lord wants to apply to your life. Ask God to move in your heart and fill you with His Spirit as you pray this. Pray for others that God is bringing to mind as you were studying this section of scripture.

DAY 3

S: Scripture. READ JOSHUA 1:7-8 (NASB)

⁷ "Only be strong and very courageous; be careful to do according to all the law which Moses My servant commanded you; do not turn from it to the right or to the left, so that you may have success wherever you go.
⁸ "This book of the law shall not depart from your mouth, but you shall meditate on it day and night, so that you may be careful to do according to all that is written in it; for then you will make your way prosperous, and then you will have success.

O: Observations. Pray and ask God to show you things in the passage and in your key verse.

Who is being talked to?

What is being said to them? (What commands are found in this passage? What warnings are given? What promises are made?)

Where is this being said or written from and is that important to what you are reading?

Are there words that are emphasized and/or being used more than once? What are the definitions of important words?

Using a tool for cross-referencing, what do other verses in the Bible add to your understanding of this verse or passage?

Looking at commentaries or Study Bible notes, what do you learn about this passage?

_____
_____
_____

How does what you learn help you understand and know God better?

_____
_____
_____

A: Application. What does this mean to you? How does this apply to your life?

_____
_____

Is there a command you should obey? Is there something you should start or stop doing? Is there a promise you should claim as a believer in Christ?

_____
_____

P: Prayer. Write out or pray based on what you have learned and what the Lord wants to apply to your life. Ask God to move in your heart and fill you with His Spirit as you pray this. Pray for others that God is bringing to mind as you were studying this section of scripture.

_____
_____
_____
_____
_____

DAY 4

S: Scripture. READ ROMANS 10:17 (NASB)
¹⁷ So faith *comes* from hearing, and hearing by the word of Christ.

O: Observations. Pray and ask God to show you things in the passage and in your key verse.
Who is being talked to?

_____

What is being said to them? (What commands are found in this passage? What warnings are given? What promises are made?)

_____

_____

Where is this being said or written from and is that important to what you are reading?

_____

_____

Are there words that are emphasized and/or being used more than once? What are the definitions of important words?

_____

_____

Using a tool for cross-referencing, what do other verses in the Bible add to your understanding of this verse or passage?

_____

_____

Looking at commentaries or Study Bible notes, what do you learn about this passage?

_____

_____

_____

How does what you learn help you understand and know God better?

A: Application. What does this mean to you? How does this apply to your life?

Is there a command you should obey? Is there something you should start or stop doing? Is there a promise you should claim as a believer in Christ?

P: Prayer. Write out or pray based on what you have learned and what the Lord wants to apply to your life. Ask God to move in your heart and fill you with His Spirit as you pray this. Pray for others that God is bringing to mind as you were studying this section of scripture.

DAY 5

S: Scripture. READ GALATIANS 3:2-5 (NASB)
² This is the only thing I want to find out from you: did you receive the Spirit by the works of the Law, or by hearing with faith? ³ Are you so foolish? Having begun by the Spirit, are you now being perfected by the flesh? ⁴ Did you suffer so many things in vain—if indeed it was in vain? ⁵ So then, does He who provides you with the Spirit and works miracles among you, do it by the works of the Law, or by hearing with faith?

O: Observations. Pray and ask God to show you things in the passage and in your key verse.

Who is being talked to?

What is being said to them? (What commands are found in this passage? What warnings are given? What promises are made?)

Where is this being said or written from and is that important to what you are reading?

Are there words that are emphasized and/or being used more than once? What are the definitions of important words?

Using a tool for cross-referencing, what do other verses in the Bible add to your understanding of this verse or passage?

Looking at commentaries or Study Bible notes, what do you learn about this passage?

_____
_____
_____

How does what you learn help you understand and know God better?

_____
_____
_____

A: Application. What does this mean to you? How does this apply to your life?

_____
_____

Is there a command you should obey? Is there something you should start or stop doing? Is there a promise you should claim as a believer in Christ?

_____
_____

P: Prayer. Write out or pray based on what you have learned and what the Lord wants to apply to your life. Ask God to move in your heart and fill you with His Spirit as you pray this. Pray for others that God is bringing to mind as you were studying this section of scripture.

_____
_____
_____
_____
_____

DAY 6

S: Scripture. READ EPHESIANS 4:11-13 (NASB)
¹¹ And He gave some as apostles, and some as prophets, and some as evangelists, and some as pastors and teachers, ¹² for the equipping of the saints for the work of service, to the building up of the body of Christ; ¹³ until we all attain to the unity of the faith, and of the knowledge of the Son of God, to a mature man, to the measure of the stature which belongs to the fullness of Christ.

O: Observations. Pray and ask God to show you things in the passage and in your key verse.
Who is being talked to?

_____

What is being said to them? (What commands are found in this passage? What warnings are given? What promises are made?)

_____

_____

Where is this being said or written from and is that important to what you are reading?

_____

_____

Are there words that are emphasized and/or being used more than once? What are the definitions of important words?

_____

_____

Using a tool for cross-referencing, what do other verses in the Bible add to your understanding of this verse or passage?

_____

_____

Looking at commentaries or Study Bible notes, what do you learn about this passage?

How does what you learn help you understand and know God better?

A: Application. What does this mean to you? How does this apply to your life?

Is there a command you should obey? Is there something you should start or stop doing? Is there a promise you should claim as a believer in Christ?

P: Prayer. Write out or pray based on what you have learned and what the Lord wants to apply to your life. Ask God to move in your heart and fill you with His Spirit as you pray this. Pray for others that God is bringing to mind as you were studying this section of scripture.

DAY 7

S: Scripture. READ AMOS 8:11-13 (NASB)
¹¹ "Behold, days are coming," declares the Lord God, "When I will send a famine on the land, not a famine for bread or a thirst for water, but rather for hearing the words of the Lord. ¹² "People will stagger from sea to sea and from the north even to the east; They will go to and fro to seek the word of the Lord, but they will not find it. ¹³ "In that day the beautiful virgins and the young men will faint from thirst.

O: Observations. Pray and ask God to show you things in the passage and in your key verse.
Who is being talked to?

What is being said to them? (What commands are found in this passage? What warnings are given? What promises are made?)

Where is this being said or written from and is that important to what you are reading?

Are there words that are emphasized and/or being used more than once? What are the definitions of important words?

Using a tool for cross-referencing, what do other verses in the Bible add to your understanding of this verse or passage?

Looking at commentaries or Study Bible notes, what do you learn about this passage?

How does what you learn help you understand and know God better?

A: Application. What does this mean to you? How does this apply to your life?

Is there a command you should obey? Is there something you should start or stop doing? Is there a promise you should claim as a believer in Christ?

P: Prayer. Write out or pray based on what you have learned and what the Lord wants to apply to your life. Ask God to move in your heart and fill you with His Spirit as you pray this. Pray for others that God is bringing to mind as you were studying this section of scripture.

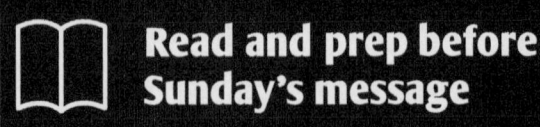

Read and prep before Sunday's message

WEEK 3

O: Obey from the Heart

Jesus told us that if we love Him then we will obey His commandments.
JOHN 14:15 (NASB) "If you love Me, you will keep My commandments.

Jesus also said that to be a disciple you need to be taught to obey all that Jesus commands.
MATTHEW 28:19-20 (NASB)
> [19] "Go therefore and make disciples of all the nations, baptizing them in the name of the Father and the Son and the Holy Spirit, [20] teaching them to observe all that I commanded you; and lo, I am with you always, even to the end of the age."

So, to go deeper in our faith and be stronger in our faith then we need to obey Jesus from the Heart. We need to obey because we love Him. If we love Him then we will want to obey Him.

When we do, our faith will increase. Faith comes by hearing and faith increases by doing. Jesus taught us this truth when the disciples came to Him and asked Him to increase their faith:

LUKE 17:5-10 (NASB)
> [5] The apostles said to the Lord, "Increase our faith!" [6] And the Lord said, "If you had faith like a mustard seed, you would say to this mulberry tree, 'Be uprooted and be planted in the sea'; and it would obey you.
> [7] "Which of you, having a slave plowing or tending sheep, will say to him when he has come in from the field, 'Come immediately and sit down to eat'? [8] "But will he not say to him, 'Prepare something for me

to eat, and properly clothe yourself and serve me while I eat and drink; and afterward you may eat and drink'? ⁹ "He does not thank the slave because he did the things which were commanded, does he?
¹⁰ "So you too, when you do all the things which are commanded you, say, 'We are unworthy slaves; we have done only that which we ought to have done.' "

When the disciples asked for Jesus to increase their faith, Jesus initially answered by telling them what faith would look like. In verse 6, what does Jesus tell them about faith and the effects of increasing faith?

What does Jesus say the master of a slave will and will not do? In verse 10, Jesus says that we need to do how much of what we are commanded? Remember, this is what Jesus says is the *key* to an increasing faith. So what is Jesus telling us will increase our faith?

Are there any commands of Jesus that you are not willing to do?

READ MATTHEW 7:24-27 (ESV)
²⁴ "Everyone then who hears these words of mine and does them will be like a wise man who built his house on the rock. ²⁵ And the rain fell, and the floods came, and the winds blew and beat on that house, but it did not fall, because it had been founded on the rock. ²⁶ And everyone who hears these words of mine and does not do them will be like a foolish man who built his house on the sand. ²⁷ And the rain fell, and the floods came, and the winds blew and beat against that house, and it fell, and great was the fall of it."

What does Jesus tell us about the person who hears His words and does them? According to Jesus, what is the key to having a strong faith?

_____

_____

What does Jesus tell us about the person who hears His words and does not do them? So how important is it for us to obey the Lord from the heart?

_____

_____

READ JOHN 14:21 (NASB)
"He who has My commandments and keeps them is the one who loves Me; and he who loves Me will be loved by My Father, and I will love him and will disclose Myself to him."

READ JOHN 14:23-24 (NASB)
²³ Jesus answered and said to him, "If anyone loves Me, he will keep My word; and My Father will love him, and We will come to him and make Our abode with him. ²⁴ "He who does not love Me does not keep My words; and the word which you hear is not Mine, but the Father's who sent Me.

According to Jesus who really loves Him and who does not love Him? What does Jesus promise to the one who loves Him and obeys His commands?

_____

_____

_____

READ 1 JOHN 5:2-4 (ESV)
² By this we know that we love the children of God, when we love God and obey His commandments. ³ For this is the love of God, that we keep His commandments. And His commandments are not burdensome. ⁴ For everyone who has been born of God overcomes the world. And this is the victory that has overcome the world—our faith.

What is the love of God according to this passage? What is the result of being born of God? How do we get victory over the world?

WEEK 3

O: Obey from the Heart: Time

The time you have to live on this earth and to live out your life purpose is a gift from God. When you see your time as a gift from God and to be used for God then your faith will increase and grow deeper.

READ PSALM 90:12 (NASB)
So teach us to number our days,
That we may present to You a heart of wisdom.

This Psalm was written by Moses and it is called the prayer of Moses. What does Moses want God to teach Him? Why do you think Moses wants God to teach him this? When you use your time correctly what will the result be?

READ ECCLESIASTES 9:10 (NASB)
Whatever your hand finds to do, do *it* with *all* your might; for there is no activity or planning or knowledge or wisdom in Sheol where you are going.

Solomon is the author of Ecclesiastes and was one of the wisest men who ever lived. And Sheol is defined as the abode of the dead, an afterlife.

What is Solomon telling us to do in this verse? Are you doing this?

_____
_____

READ JOHN 9:4 (NASB)

We must work the works of Him who sent Me as long as it is day; night is coming when no one can work.

Jesus is speaking here. What does Jesus say we should do? How does this apply to using your time? Are you using your time to serve God?

_____
_____

READ EPHESIANS 5:15-17 (NASB)

15 Therefore be careful how you walk, not as unwise men but as wise, 16 making the most of your time, because the days are evil. 17 So then do not be foolish, but understand what the will of the Lord is.

Paul is writing to the church in Ephesus here. What can we learn to do in this passage? What is the difference between a wise person and a fool?

_____

Are you making God a priority when it comes to the use of your time? Does your weekly schedule show that God gets the time He would want you to give Him?

_____
_____

WEEK 3
O: Obey from the Heart: Talent

Every Christian has been given a Spiritual gift that God wants them to use in serving Him in the Church. This gift is chosen by the Holy Spirit and given to you because it fits you. This is a huge part of how you fulfill your God given purpose. The result of using your gift is specific joy that comes from fulfilling your purpose.

1 CORINTHIANS 12:7 (NLT)
A spiritual gift is given to each of us so we can help each other.

1 CORINTHIANS 12:11 (NLT)
It is the one and only Spirit who distributes all these gifts. He alone decides which gift each person should have.

ROMANS 12:6A (NLT)
In His grace, God has given us different gifts for doing certain things well.

What is given to each of us by the Holy Spirit? Why is this given to each one of us? Who decides what spiritual gift you get?

_____

Do you know what your spiritual gift is? Are you using your spiritual gift?

_____

READ ROMANS 1:11-12 (NLT)
¹¹ For I long to visit you so I can bring you some spiritual gift that will help you grow strong in the Lord. ¹² When we get together, I want to encourage you in your faith, but I also want to be encouraged by yours.

Paul is writing to the church in Rome; what did he want to use his spiritual gift to accomplish with them? What does this tell you a spiritual gift is for? Are you using your spiritual gift for the same purpose and seeing the results using it to encourage others?

_____
_____

How does using your spiritual gift tie in to obeying God from the heart in the use of your time?

_____
_____

To discover your spiritual gift(s), visit:
www.CrossroadsChurch.com/growjournal

What are your top three Spiritual Gifts?

_____

Do you see that using these three gifts to minister to others in the Church would be something you would love? Are you now using your gift or gifts? If not, make a commitment to find a place in the Church to use your gift so you will truly be obeying God from the heart.

_____
_____

READ MATTHEW 25:14-30 (NASB)

[14] "For it is just like a man about to go on a journey, who called his own slaves and entrusted his possessions to them. [15] "To one he gave five talents, to another, two, and to another, one, each according to his own ability; and he went on his journey. [16] "Immediately the one who had received the five talents went and traded with them, and gained five more talents. [17] "In the same manner the one who had received the two talents gained two more. [18] "But he who received the one talent went away, and dug a hole in the ground and hid his master's money.

19 "Now after a long time the master of those slaves came and settled accounts with them. **20** "The one who had received the five talents came up and brought five more talents, saying, 'Master, you entrusted five talents to me. See, I have gained five more talents.' **21** "His master said to him, 'Well done, good and faithful slave. You were faithful with a few things, I will put you in charge of many things; enter into the joy of your master.'

22 "Also the one who had received the two talents came up and said, 'Master, you entrusted two talents to me. See, I have gained two more talents.' **23** "His master said to him, 'Well done, good and faithful slave. You were faithful with a few things, I will put you in charge of many things; enter into the joy of your master.'

24 "And the one also who had received the one talent came up and said, 'Master, I knew you to be a hard man, reaping where you did not sow and gathering where you scattered no seed. **25** 'And I was afraid, and went away and hid your talent in the ground. See, you have what is yours.'

26 "But his master answered and said to him, 'You wicked, lazy slave, you knew that I reap where I did not sow and gather where I scattered no seed. **27** 'Then you ought to have put my money in the bank, and on my arrival I would have received my money back with interest. **28** 'Therefore take away the talent from him, and give it to the one who has the ten talents.'

29 "For to everyone who has, more shall be given, and he will have an abundance; but from the one who does not have, even what he does have shall be taken away. **30** "Throw out the worthless slave into the outer darkness; in that place there will be weeping and gnashing of teeth.

Talent was a monetary currency in the day of Jesus. Jesus uses it in this parable to represent the spiritual gift God gives you.

What do you learn about the amount of talent that God gave different people and why? What is the amount of talent given according to?

What did the Lord expect each person to do with their talents?
What is the reward Jesus will give to the ones who use them the way they are supposed to?

_____

_____

What is the judgment Jesus pronounces on the one who does not use the talent Jesus gave them, but buries it instead? What does this tell you about the seriousness of your obeying Jesus from the heart in the use of your Spiritual gift(s)?

_____

_____

Along with your Spiritual gifts, God gave you talents that are a big part of your God-given identity and purpose. God endowed you with these talents and God wants to empower you to use these talents. When you use these talents to fulfill your God given purpose, your life will have a deep and truly everlasting meaning.

Talents can be…
- Singing
- Playing musical instruments
- Writing
- Cooking
- Cleaning.
- Craftsmanship
- Construction
- Acting and performing arts
- Computer programming
- Organization
- Public Speaking
- And so much more…

LOOK AT EXODUS 28:3 (NASB)
"You shall speak to all the skillful persons whom I have endowed with the spirit of wisdom, that they make Aaron's garments to consecrate him, that he may minister as priest to Me.

AND EXODUS 31:2-6 (NASB)

² "See, I have called by name Bezalel, the son of Uri, the son of Hur, of the tribe of Judah. ³ "I have filled him with the Spirit of God in wisdom, in understanding, in knowledge, and in all kinds of craftsmanship, ⁴ to make artistic designs for work in gold, in silver, and in bronze, ⁵ and in the cutting of stones for settings, and in the carving of wood, that he may work in all kinds of craftsmanship. ⁶ "And behold, I Myself have appointed with him Oholiab, the son of Ahisamach, of the tribe of Dan; and in the hearts of all who are skillful I have put skill, that they may make all that I have commanded you:

What talent did God give each of the people mentioned here?

_____

_____

What talents has God given you?

_____

_____

Sermon notes

Hear the message and take notes

DATE: November 13th

SERMON TITLE:

SPEAKER:

Study and dig deeper on your own

Use the SOAP method to review the scriptures we studied in the Obey from the heart - Time & Talent sections

DAY 1

S: Scripture. JOHN 14:15 (NASB)
¹⁵ "If you love Me, you will keep My commandments.

O: Observations. Pray and ask God to show you things in the passage and in your key verse.
Who is being talked to?

What is being said to them? (What commands are found in this passage? What warnings are given? What promises are made?)

Where is this being said or written from and is that important to what you are reading?

Are there words that are emphasized and/or being used more than once? What are the definitions of important words?

Using a tool for cross-referencing, what do other verses in the Bible add to your understanding of this verse or passage?

Looking at commentaries or Study Bible notes, what do you learn about this passage?

_____
_____
_____

How does what you learn help you understand and know God better?

_____
_____
_____

A: Application. What does this mean to you? How does this apply to your life?

_____
_____

Is there a command you should obey? Is there something you should start or stop doing? Is there a promise you should claim as a believer in Christ?

_____
_____

P: Prayer. Write out or pray based on what you have learned and what the Lord wants to apply to your life. Ask God to move in your heart and fill you with His Spirit as you pray this. Pray for others that God is bringing to mind as you were studying this section of scripture.

_____
_____
_____
_____
_____

DAY 2

S: Scripture. LUKE 17:5-10 (NASB)

⁵ The apostles said to the Lord, "Increase our faith!" ⁶ And the Lord said, "If you had faith like a mustard seed, you would say to this mulberry tree, 'Be uprooted and be planted in the sea'; and it would obey you. ⁷ "Which of you, having a slave plowing or tending sheep, will say to him when he has come in from the field, 'Come immediately and sit down to eat'? ⁸ "But will he not say to him, 'Prepare something for me to eat, and properly clothe yourself and serve me while I eat and drink; and afterward you may eat and drink'? ⁹ "He does not thank the slave because he did the things which were commanded, does he? ¹⁰ "So you too, when you do all the things which are commanded you, say, 'We are unworthy slaves; we have done only that which we ought to have done.'

O: Observations. Pray and ask God to show you things in the passage and in your key verse.

Who is being talked to?

_____

What is being said to them? (What commands are found in this passage? What warnings are given? What promises are made?)

_____

_____

Where is this being said or written from and is that important to what you are reading?

_____

_____

Are there words that are emphasized and/or being used more than once? What are the definitions of important words?

_____

_____

Using a tool for cross-referencing, what do other verses in the Bible add to your understanding of this verse or passage?

Looking at commentaries or Study Bible notes, what do you learn about this passage?

How does what you learn help you understand and know God better?

A: Application. What does this mean to you? How does this apply to your life?

Is there a command you should obey? Is there something you should start or stop doing? Is there a promise you should claim as a believer in Christ?

P: Prayer. Write out or pray based on what you have learned and what the Lord wants to apply to your life. Ask God to move in your heart and fill you with His Spirit as you pray this. Pray for others that God is bringing to mind as you were studying this section of scripture.

DAY 3

S: Scripture. READ MATTHEW 7:24-27 (ESV)
24 "Everyone then who hears these words of mine and does them will be like a wise man who built his house on the rock. 25 And the rain fell, and the floods came, and the winds blew and beat on that house, but it did not fall, because it had been founded on the rock. 26 And everyone who hears these words of mine and does not do them will be like a foolish man who built his house on the sand. 27 And the rain fell, and the floods came, and the winds blew and beat against that house, and it fell, and great was the fall of it."

O: Observations. Pray and ask God to show you things in the passage and in your key verse.
Who is being talked to?

What is being said to them? (What commands are found in this passage? What warnings are given? What promises are made?)

Where is this being said or written from and is that important to what you are reading?

Are there words that are emphasized and/or being used more than once? What are the definitions of important words?

Using a tool for cross-referencing, what do other verses in the Bible add to your understanding of this verse or passage?

Looking at commentaries or Study Bible notes, what do you learn about this passage?

How does what you learn help you understand and know God better?

A: Application. What does this mean to you? How does this apply to your life?

Is there a command you should obey? Is there something you should start or stop doing? Is there a promise you should claim as a believer in Christ?

P: Prayer. Write out or pray based on what you have learned and what the Lord wants to apply to your life. Ask God to move in your heart and fill you with His Spirit as you pray this. Pray for others that God is bringing to mind as you were studying this section of scripture.

DAY 4

S: Scripture. READ JOHN 9:4 (NASB)
⁴ We must work the works of Him who sent Me as long as it is day; night is coming when no one can work.

O: Observations. Pray and ask God to show you things in the passage and in your key verse.
Who is being talked to?

What is being said to them? (What commands are found in this passage? What warnings are given? What promises are made?)

Where is this being said or written from and is that important to what you are reading?

Are there words that are emphasized and/or being used more than once? What are the definitions of important words?

Using a tool for cross-referencing, what do other verses in the Bible add to your understanding of this verse or passage?

Looking at commentaries or Study Bible notes, what do you learn about this passage?

How does what you learn help you understand and know God better?

A: Application. What does this mean to you? How does this apply to your life?

Is there a command you should obey? Is there something you should start or stop doing? Is there a promise you should claim as a believer in Christ?

P: Prayer. Write out or pray based on what you have learned and what the Lord wants to apply to your life. Ask God to move in your heart and fill you with His Spirit as you pray this. Pray for others that God is bringing to mind as you were studying this section of scripture.

DAY 5

S: Scripture. READ EPHESIANS 5:15-17 (NASB)
¹⁵ Therefore be careful how you walk, not as unwise men but as wise, ¹⁶ making the most of your time, because the days are evil. ¹⁷ So then do not be foolish, but understand what the will of the Lord is.

O: Observations. Pray and ask God to show you things in the passage and in your key verse.
Who is being talked to?

_____

What is being said to them? (What commands are found in this passage? What warnings are given? What promises are made?)

_____

_____

Where is this being said or written from and is that important to what you are reading?

_____

_____

Are there words that are emphasized and/or being used more than once? What are the definitions of important words?

_____

_____

Using a tool for cross-referencing, what do other verses in the Bible add to your understanding of this verse or passage?

_____

_____

Looking at commentaries or Study Bible notes, what do you learn about this passage?

_____
_____
_____

How does what you learn help you understand and know God better?

_____
_____
_____

A: Application. What does this mean to you? How does this apply to your life?

_____
_____
_____

Is there a command you should obey? Is there something you should start or stop doing? Is there a promise you should claim as a believer in Christ?

_____
_____

P: Prayer. Write out or pray based on what you have learned and what the Lord wants to apply to your life. Ask God to move in your heart and fill you with His Spirit as you pray this. Pray for others that God is bringing to mind as you were studying this section of scripture.

_____
_____
_____
_____
_____
_____

DAY 6

S: Scripture. 1 CORINTHIANS 12:11 (NLT)
11 It is the one and only Spirit who distributes all these gifts. He alone decides which gift each person should have.

O: Observations. Pray and ask God to show you things in the passage and in your key verse.
Who is being talked to?

___

What is being said to them? (What commands are found in this passage? What warnings are given? What promises are made?)

___

___

Where is this being said or written from and is that important to what you are reading?

___

___

Are there words that are emphasized and/or being used more than once? What are the definitions of important words?

___

___

Using a tool for cross-referencing, what do other verses in the Bible add to your understanding of this verse or passage?

___

___

Looking at commentaries or Study Bible notes, what do you learn about this passage?

___

___

How does what you learn help you understand and know God better?

A: Application. What does this mean to you? How does this apply to your life?

Is there a command you should obey? Is there something you should start or stop doing? Is there a promise you should claim as a believer in Christ?

P: Prayer. Write out or pray based on what you have learned and what the Lord wants to apply to your life. Ask God to move in your heart and fill you with His Spirit as you pray this. Pray for others that God is bringing to mind as you were studying this section of scripture.

DAY 7

S: Scripture. READ ROMANS 1:11-12 (NLT)
¹¹ For I long to visit you so I can bring you some spiritual gift that will help you grow strong in the Lord. ¹² When we get together, I want to encourage you in your faith, but I also want to be encouraged by yours.

O: Observations. Pray and ask God to show you things in the passage and in your key verse.
Who is being talked to?

_____

What is being said to them? (What commands are found in this passage? What warnings are given? What promises are made?)

_____
_____

Where is this being said or written from and is that important to what you are reading?

_____
_____

Are there words that are emphasized and/or being used more than once? What are the definitions of important words?

_____
_____

Using a tool for cross-referencing, what do other verses in the Bible add to your understanding of this verse or passage?

_____
_____

Looking at commentaries or Study Bible notes, what do you learn about this passage?

_____
_____

How does what you learn help you understand and know God better?

A: Application. What does this mean to you? How does this apply to your life?

Is there a command you should obey? Is there something you should start or stop doing? Is there a promise you should claim as a believer in Christ?

P: Prayer. Write out or pray based on what you have learned and what the Lord wants to apply to your life. Ask God to move in your heart and fill you with His Spirit as you pray this. Pray for others that God is bringing to mind as you were studying this section of scripture.

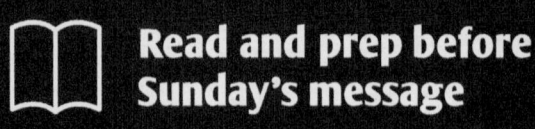

Read and prep before Sunday's message

WEEK 4

O: Obey from the Heart: Treasure

Jesus taught us that where our treasure is, there our heart will be also.

MATTHEW 6:21 (NLT) "Wherever your treasure is, there the desires of your heart will also be."

If your heart is with the Lord, if you love the Lord then you will obey from the heart and give to the Lord. The Bible teaches we will give the tithe which is the first ten percent of any income that you receive. The Bible also teaches and calls for us to give God offerings beyond the tithe based on how He has blessed us.

God tells us to come and give to Him based on the way He has blessed us and we are not to come bringing nothing.

READ DEUTERONOMY 16:16-17 (NASB)
¹⁶ "Three times in a year all your males shall appear before the Lord your God in the place which He chooses, at the Feast of Unleavened Bread and at the Feast of Weeks and at the Feast of Booths, and they shall not appear before the Lord empty-handed. ¹⁷ "Every man shall give as he is able, according to the blessing of the Lord your God which He has given you.

Are you being faithful in giving to God the tithe and the offering based on how He has blessed you?

_____

_____

_____

READ MATTHEW 23:23C (NLT)
You should tithe, yes, but do not neglect the more important things."

AND LUKE 6:38 (NLT)
Give, and you will receive. Your gift will return to you in full—pressed down, shaken together to make room for more, running over, and poured into your lap. The amount you give will determine the amount you get back.

What does Jesus tell us we should do? What does Jesus promise will happen when we are faithful in obeying Him from the heart?

READ MALACHI 3:6-11 (NASB)
⁶ "For I, the Lord, do not change; therefore you, O sons of Jacob, are not consumed. ⁷ "From the days of your fathers you have turned aside from My statutes and have not kept them. Return to Me, and I will return to you," says the Lord of hosts. "But you say, 'How shall we return?' ⁸ "Will a man rob God? Yet you are robbing Me! But you say, 'How have we robbed You?' In tithes and offerings. ⁹ "You are cursed with a curse, for you are robbing Me, the whole nation of you! ¹⁰ "Bring the whole tithe into the storehouse, so that there may be food in My house, and test Me now in this," says the Lord of hosts, "if I will not open for you the windows of heaven and pour out for you a blessing until it overflows. ¹¹ "Then I will rebuke the devourer for you, so that it will not destroy the fruits of the ground; nor will your vine in the field cast its grapes," says the Lord of hosts.

What does God tell us about Himself? Why is this important for you to know? What does God say we are doing if we do not tithe? What is the result of not tithing?

What is God telling us to do? What does God promise if we will be faithful and obey from the heart?

_____
_____

READ PROVERBS 3:9-12 (NASB)
⁹ Honor the Lord from your wealth And from the first of all your produce; ¹⁰ So your barns will be filled with plenty And your vats will overflow with new wine. ¹¹ My son, do not reject the discipline of the Lord Or loathe His reproof, ¹² For whom the Lord loves He reproves, Even as a father corrects the son in whom he delights.

How are we told to honor God? Why is it important we give to God first? What does God promise to do for us if we are faithful in honoring Him?

_____
_____
_____

Jesus wants you to obey all of His commands and He wants you to obey from the heart. Take time to pray and commit to being faithful in obeying from the heart in the area of your treasure (your finances). Commit to giving the whole tithe to God.

Pray and ask God how much He is going to bless you with so you can give an offering to Him. Ask God to bring to mind how much that will be this year. Then, as the year comes to pass, see if God blesses you so much that you will be able to give that amount of offering to Him.

Write down how much your tithe this year will be (Income x 10%) :

_____

Write down how much your offering will be above your tithe:

_____

WEEK 4
O: Obey from the Heart: Testimony

In Revelation 12 we see the moment that we as Believers are completely victorious over the Devil, our greatest enemy. And in that moment we are told what it is that brings us the victory.

READ REVELATION 12:10-11 (NASB)
> ¹⁰ Then I heard a loud voice in heaven, saying, "Now the salvation, and the power, and the kingdom of our God and the authority of His Christ have come, for the accuser of our brethren has been thrown down, he who accuses them before our God day and night. ¹¹ "And they overcame him because of the blood of the Lamb and because of the word of their testimony, and they did not love their life even when faced with death.

What are the three reasons we overcome the Devil according to verse 11?

_____

_____

_____

Note the second thing that is listed that gives us victory is "the word of their testimony." This means that you are to have a "testimony" of what Jesus has done and is doing in your life that you can share. GROW is how you deepen and strengthen your faith. When you do this then you will be living in the power of God and moving in the way of miracles. And you will have a testimony to share. And when you obey from the heart then you will be so filled with the Holy Spirit that you will want to share your testimony.

READ MATTHEW 28:18-20 (NASB)
> ¹⁸ And Jesus came up and spoke to them, saying, "All authority has been given to Me in heaven and on earth. ¹⁹ "Go therefore and make disciples

of all the nations, baptizing them in the name of the Father and the Son and the Holy Spirit, ²⁰ teaching them to observe all that I commanded you; and lo, I am with you always, even to the end of the age."

READ ACTS 1:8 (NASB)
"...but you will receive power when the Holy Spirit has come upon you; and you shall be My witnesses both in Jerusalem, and in all Judea and Samaria, and even to the remotest part of the earth."

What does Jesus tell us we are to do? What does Jesus tell us we are to be? Where does Jesus say we are to do this? Are you praying for opportunities to share your faith (testimony) in Jesus? Who are you seeking to share with?

READ JOHN 4:28-29 (NASB)
²⁸ So the woman left her waterpot, and went into the city and said to the men, ²⁹ "Come, see a man who told me all the things that I have done; this is not the Christ, is it?"

READ JOHN 4:39 (NASB)
From that city many of the Samaritans believed in Him because of the word of the woman who testified, "He told me all the things that I have done."

We call **this woman the woman at the well** because Jesus had a divine appointment with her at a well in Samaria at noon. What does the woman do after she has this encounter with Jesus? What does she tell the people she goes to about Jesus and what He did in her life? What is the result?

READ JOHN 9:25 (NASB)

He then answered, "Whether He is a sinner, I do not know; one thing I do know, that though I was blind, now I see."

This occurs after Jesus healed a man who had been blind from birth. The miracle could not be denied but the Pharisees were denying that Jesus is the Christ. When they question the man who has been healed, what does he tell the Pharisees?

_____
_____

Reflect on the power of these two testimonies.

_____
_____
_____
_____

Now list some things that Jesus has done in your life. What are some prayers that He answered? Was there a time He revealed things to you? When did Jesus intercede for you? Was there a time Jesus turned something to good in your life?

_____
_____
_____
_____

A way to write out your testimony so it is ready to be shared with others is by following this formula: Before Christ, something happened, now what?

Before Christ - how was your life before Christ?

_____
_____
_____
_____
_____
_____

Something happened - what happened in your life that made you encounter Jesus and become a Christian?

_____
_____
_____
_____
_____
_____

Now what - how is your life now that you are living your life with Jesus?

_____
_____
_____
_____
_____
_____
_____

Make a prayer list of people in your life who do not know Jesus. Pray that their hearts would be softened to accept Jesus as their Lord and Savior. Pray for an opportunity to share your testimony with them.

1.
2.
3.
4.
5.
6.
7.
8.
9.
10.
11.
12.
13.
14.
15.
16.
17.
18.
19.
20.

Hear the message and take notes

Sermon notes

DATE
November 20th

SERMON TITLE

SPEAKER

Study and dig deeper on your own

Use the SOAP method to review the scriptures we studied in the Obey from the heart - Treasure & Testimony sections

DAY 1

S: Scripture. READ DEUTERONOMY 16:16-17 (NASB)

¹⁶ "Three times in a year all your males shall appear before the Lord your God in the place which He chooses, at the Feast of Unleavened Bread and at the Feast of Weeks and at the Feast of Booths, and they shall not appear before the Lord empty-handed. ¹⁷ "Every man shall give as he is able, according to the blessing of the Lord your God which He has given you.

O: Observations. Pray and ask God to show you things in the passage and in your key verse.

Who is being talked to?

What is being said to them? (What commands are found in this passage? What warnings are given? What promises are made?)

Where is this being said or written from and is that important to what you are reading?

Are there words that are emphasized and/or being used more than once? What are the definitions of important words?

Using a tool for cross-referencing, what do other verses in the Bible add to your understanding of this verse or passage?

Looking at commentaries or Study Bible notes, what do you learn about this passage?

How does what you learn help you understand and know God better?

A: Application. What does this mean to you? How does this apply to your life?

Is there a command you should obey? Is there something you should start or stop doing? Is there a promise you should claim as a believer in Christ?

P: Prayer. Write out or pray based on what you have learned and what the Lord wants to apply to your life. Ask God to move in your heart and fill you with His Spirit as you pray this. Pray for others that God is bringing to mind as you were studying this section of scripture.

DAY 2

S: Scripture. MATTHEW 23:23 (NLT)
²³ "What sorrow awaits you teachers of religious law and you Pharisees. Hypocrites! For you are careful to tithe even the tiniest income from your herb gardens, but you ignore the more important aspects of the law—justice, mercy, and faith. You should tithe, yes, but do not neglect the more important things.

O: Observations. Pray and ask God to show you things in the passage and in your key verse.
Who is being talked to?

_____
_____

What is being said to them? (What commands are found in this passage? What warnings are given? What promises are made?)

_____
_____

Where is this being said or written from and is that important to what you are reading?

_____
_____

Are there words that are emphasized and/or being used more than once? What are the definitions of important words?

_____
_____

Using a tool for cross-referencing, what do other verses in the Bible add to your understanding of this verse or passage?

_____
_____

Looking at commentaries or Study Bible notes, what do you learn about this passage?

_____
_____
_____

How does what you learn help you understand and know God better?

_____
_____
_____

A: Application. What does this mean to you? How does this apply to your life?

_____
_____

Is there a command you should obey? Is there something you should start or stop doing? Is there a promise you should claim as a believer in Christ?

_____
_____

P: Prayer. Write out or pray based on what you have learned and what the Lord wants to apply to your life. Ask God to move in your heart and fill you with His Spirit as you pray this. Pray for others that God is bringing to mind as you were studying this section of scripture.

_____
_____
_____
_____
_____

DAY 3

S: Scripture. LUKE 6:38 (NLT)
³⁸ Give, and you will receive. Your gift will return to you in full—pressed down, shaken together to make room for more, running over, and poured into your lap. The amount you give will determine the amount you get back.

O: Observations. Pray and ask God to show you things in the passage and in your key verse.

Who is being talked to?

_____

_____

What is being said to them? (What commands are found in this passage? What warnings are given? What promises are made?)

_____

_____

Where is this being said or written from and is that important to what you are reading?

_____

_____

Are there words that are emphasized and/or being used more than once? What are the definitions of important words?

_____

_____

Using a tool for cross-referencing, what do other verses in the Bible add to your understanding of this verse or passage?

_____

_____

Looking at commentaries or Study Bible notes, what do you learn about this passage?

_____
_____
_____

How does what you learn help you understand and know God better?

_____
_____
_____

A: Application. What does this mean to you? How does this apply to your life?

_____
_____

Is there a command you should obey? Is there something you should start or stop doing? Is there a promise you should claim as a believer in Christ?

_____
_____

P: Prayer. Write out or pray based on what you have learned and what the Lord wants to apply to your life. Ask God to move in your heart and fill you with His Spirit as you pray this. Pray for others that God is bringing to mind as you were studying this section of scripture.

_____
_____
_____
_____
_____
_____

DAY 4

S: Scripture. READ MALACHI 3:6-11 (NASB)

6 "For I, the Lord, do not change; therefore you, O sons of Jacob, are not consumed. 7 "From the days of your fathers you have turned aside from My statutes and have not kept them. Return to Me, and I will return to you," says the Lord of hosts. "But you say, 'How shall we return?' 8 "Will a man rob God? Yet you are robbing Me! But you say, 'How have we robbed You?' In tithes and offerings. 9 "You are cursed with a curse, for you are robbing Me, the whole nation of you! 10 "Bring the whole tithe into the storehouse, so that there may be food in My house, and test Me now in this," says the Lord of hosts, "if I will not open for you the windows of heaven and pour out for you a blessing until it overflows.
11 "Then I will rebuke the devourer for you, so that it will not destroy the fruits of the ground; nor will your vine in the field cast its grapes," says the Lord of hosts.

O: Observations. Pray and ask God to show you things in the passage and in your key verse.

Who is being talked to?

_____

_____

What is being said to them? (What commands are found in this passage? What warnings are given? What promises are made?)

_____

_____

Where is this being said or written from and is that important to what you are reading?

_____

_____

Are there words that are emphasized and/or being used more than once? What are the definitions of important words?

_____

_____

Using a tool for cross-referencing, what do other verses in the Bible add to your understanding of this verse or passage?

Looking at commentaries or Study Bible notes, what do you learn about this passage?

How does what you learn help you understand and know God better?

A: Application. What does this mean to you? How does this apply to your life?

Is there a command you should obey? Is there something you should start or stop doing? Is there a promise you should claim as a believer in Christ?

P: Prayer. Write out or pray based on what you have learned and what the Lord wants to apply to your life. Ask God to move in your heart and fill you with His Spirit as you pray this. Pray for others that God is bringing to mind as you were studying this section of scripture.

DAY 5

S: Scripture. READ REVELATION 12:10-11 (NASB)

¹⁰ Then I heard a loud voice in heaven, saying, "Now the salvation, and the power, and the kingdom of our God and the authority of His Christ have come, for the accuser of our brethren has been thrown down, he who accuses them before our God day and night. ¹¹ "And they overcame him because of the blood of the Lamb and because of the word of their testimony, and they did not love their life even when faced with death.

O: Observations. Pray and ask God to show you things in the passage and in your key verse.

Who is being talked to?

What is being said to them? (What commands are found in this passage? What warnings are given? What promises are made?)

Where is this being said or written from and is that important to what you are reading?

Are there words that are emphasized and/or being used more than once? What are the definitions of important words?

Using a tool for cross-referencing, what do other verses in the Bible add to your understanding of this verse or passage?

Looking at commentaries or Study Bible notes, what do you learn about this passage?

_____
_____
_____

How does what you learn help you understand and know God better?

_____
_____
_____

A: Application. What does this mean to you? How does this apply to your life?

_____
_____

Is there a command you should obey? Is there something you should start or stop doing? Is there a promise you should claim as a believer in Christ?

_____
_____

P: Prayer. Write out or pray based on what you have learned and what the Lord wants to apply to your life. Ask God to move in your heart and fill you with His Spirit as you pray this. Pray for others that God is bringing to mind as you were studying this section of scripture.

_____
_____
_____
_____
_____

DAY 6

S: Scripture. READ ACTS 1:8 (NASB)
⁸ "…but you will receive power when the Holy Spirit has come upon you; and you shall be My witnesses both in Jerusalem, and in all Judea and Samaria, and even to the remotest part of the earth."

O: Observations. Pray and ask God to show you things in the passage and in your key verse.
Who is being talked to?

_____

What is being said to them? (What commands are found in this passage? What warnings are given? What promises are made?)

_____

_____

Where is this being said or written from and is that important to what you are reading?

_____

_____

Are there words that are emphasized and/or being used more than once? What are the definitions of important words?

_____

_____

Using a tool for cross-referencing, what do other verses in the Bible add to your understanding of this verse or passage?

_____

_____

Looking at commentaries or Study Bible notes, what do you learn about this passage?

_____

_____

_____

How does what you learn help you understand and know God better?

A: Application. What does this mean to you? How does this apply to your life?

Is there a command you should obey? Is there something you should start or stop doing? Is there a promise you should claim as a believer in Christ?

P: Prayer. Write out or pray based on what you have learned and what the Lord wants to apply to your life. Ask God to move in your heart and fill you with His Spirit as you pray this. Pray for others that God is bringing to mind as you were studying this section of scripture.

DAY 7

S: Scripture. READ JOHN 4:28–29 (NASB)
²⁸ So the woman left her waterpot, and went into the city and said to the men, ²⁹ "Come, see a man who told me all the things that I have done; this is not the Christ, is it?"

READ JOHN 4:39 (NASB)
³⁹ From that city many of the Samaritans believed in Him because of the word of the woman who testified, "He told me all the things that I have done."

O: Observations. Pray and ask God to show you things in the passage and in your key verse.
Who is being talked to?

What is being said to them? (What commands are found in this passage? What warnings are given? What promises are made?)

Where is this being said or written from and is that important to what you are reading?

Are there words that are emphasized and/or being used more than once? What are the definitions of important words?

Using a tool for cross-referencing, what do other verses in the Bible add to your understanding of this verse or passage?

Looking at commentaries or Study Bible notes, what do you learn about this passage?

How does what you learn help you understand and know God better?

A: Application. What does this mean to you? How does this apply to your life?

Is there a command you should obey? Is there something you should start or stop doing? Is there a promise you should claim as a believer in Christ?

P: Prayer. Write out or pray based on what you have learned and what the Lord wants to apply to your life. Ask God to move in your heart and fill you with His Spirit as you pray this. Pray for others that God is bringing to mind as you were studying this section of scripture.

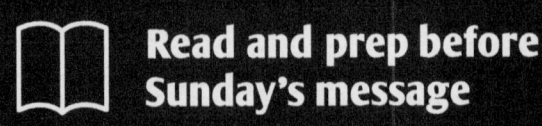

WEEK 5

W: Worship with Passion

The "W" in GROW stands for Worship and we are calling for you to commit to passionately worshiping with the Crossroads family on every First Wednesday of each month for the next three years. You can be with us in person or you can join us online.

If you can't do this on Wednesday, then you can join the Worship service at a time that works for you by viewing the service on-demand on our YouTube page. Subscribe to our page at **www.CrossroadsChurch.com/growjournal** so you don't miss a service.

Worshiping God is the act of a disciple who desires to give God glory and draw close to Him. Worship is how we enter into His presence in a special way. Worship is one way we wage Spiritual warfare and find victory. Worship is a way we show our love for God and draw close to Him to experience His love.

There are many ways we worship God and one that is vital is by coming together with other believers and worshiping together.

The two most used words for Praise in the Bible are *"Hallel"* and *"Yadah."*

Hallel means "to act clamorously foolish." The word has the idea of worshiping with such passion that others can see your love for God in a passionate and visible way.

Yadah means "to extend the hand." When we worship this way we lift our hands to the Lord asking for Him to come near to us and lift us up. It is much like when a child runs to you and lifts their hands to you wanting you to pick them up and hold them.

READ PSALM 89:15-17 (NLT)

> [15] Happy are those who hear the joyful call to worship, for they will walk in the light of your presence, Lord. [16] They rejoice all day long in your wonderful reputation. They exult in your righteousness. [17] You are their glorious strength. It pleases you to make us strong.

While you can worship anywhere and can worship on your own, this Psalm is about those who hear and heed the call to come together with the community of believers to worship God.

There are 6 Promises in this passage for those who Heed the call to come together and Worship, what are they? Which of the promises have you found to be true when you worship God?

1.
2.
3.
4.
5.
6.

READ PSALM 100:1-5 (NLT)

> [1] Shout with joy to the Lord, all the earth! [2] Worship the Lord with gladness. Come before him, singing with joy. [3] Acknowledge that the Lord is God! He made us, and we are His. We are His people, the sheep of his pasture. [4] Enter His gates with thanksgiving; go into His courts with praise. Give thanks to Him and praise His name. [5] For the Lord is good. His unfailing love continues forever, and His faithfulness continues to each generation.

We are told here that we enter into God's presence with Worship. Again, this Psalm is about coming together with other believers to worship God with them. How are we told to worship God in this Psalm? Have you worshiped God in this way? What happened when you did?

Worship Pathways

A spiritual pathway can be described as the way I most naturally connect with or experience God. We are going to explain seven pathways to experience God, and you may have a top 2 where you experience God.

1. **The first pathway is Worship.** If this is one of your top two, you probably have a natural gift for expression and celebration. "Music is my life", may be your mantra. Guard against judging those who are not as expressive as you. Resist the tendency to only look for the next "worship high."
2. **The second pathway is Contemplation.** If this is you... you have a large inner world and feel close to God when you are alone and distractions are removed. You think big thoughts about life. But, be careful, in times of stress you feel the need to retreat. Let acts of service and genuine relationships keep you tethered to the real world.
3. **The third pathway is Serving.** If this is your pathway, you experience joy through serving. God's presence is real to you when you're helping other people. Sometimes you wonder why everyone isn't serving and a bit of resentment can creep in. But, in the end, you know that you are most like Jesus when you serve.
4. **The fourth pathway is Intellectual.** If this is your pathway, the more you learn about God, the closer you feel and the more you appreciate Him. Whether it is reviewing archaeological evidence for the Bible or reading a Christian commentary, you love learning about Him. You've found God's way to your heart is through your mind. In times of crisis you might go into problem solving mode too quickly, worry, or over-analyze, instead of praying.
5. **The fifth pathway is Relational.** Being with people makes you happy and talking about the spiritual truths, engages you. You have a deep sense of God's presence when you're involved in significant relationships. Guard against being "spread too thin". Don't lose your own identity by becoming a spiritual chameleon and caring too much about what others think of you.

6. **The sixth pathway is Creation.** You love the outdoors. It wouldn't be unusual if you choose an occupation working with your hands or that places you outside most of the day. You might say you feel like you "connect with God when you are experiencing the world that He has made." In times of stress, pressure, or life transitions, don't allow the pathway to become an escape from relating to people.
7. **The seventh is Activist.** If this is your pathway, you are passionate... maybe too passionate about some things. You are keenly aware of when God is mobilizing people to address an injustice or important cause. Let your zeal be conditioned so you don't exploit people in your pursuits.

What are your top 2 pathways to experience God?

_____

_____

Sermon notes

Hear the message and take notes

DATE: November 27th

SERMON TITLE:

SPEAKER:

Study and dig deeper on your own

Use the SOAP method to review the scriptures we studied in the Worship section

DAY 1

S: Scripture. READ PSALM 89:15-17 (NLT)
¹⁵ Happy are those who hear the joyful call to worship, for they will walk in the light of your presence, Lord. ¹⁶ They rejoice all day long in your wonderful reputation. They exult in your righteousness. ¹⁷ You are their glorious strength. It pleases you to make us strong.

O: Observations. Pray and ask God to show you things in the passage and in your key verse.
Who is being talked to?

___

What is being said to them? (What commands are found in this passage? What warnings are given? What promises are made?)

___

Where is this being said or written from and is that important to what you are reading?

___

Are there words that are emphasized and/or being used more than once? What are the definitions of important words?

___

Using a tool for cross-referencing, what do other verses in the Bible add to your understanding of this verse or passage?

___

Looking at commentaries or Study Bible notes, what do you learn about this passage?

How does what you learn help you understand and know God better?

A: Application. What does this mean to you? How does this apply to your life?

Is there a command you should obey? Is there something you should start or stop doing? Is there a promise you should claim as a believer in Christ?

P: Prayer. Write out or pray based on what you have learned and what the Lord wants to apply to your life. Ask God to move in your heart and fill you with His Spirit as you pray this. Pray for others that God is bringing to mind as you were studying this section of scripture.

DAY 2

S: Scripture. READ PSALM 100:1–5 (NLT)
¹ Shout with joy to the Lord, all the earth! ² Worship the Lord with gladness. Come before him, singing with joy. ³ Acknowledge that the Lord is God! He made us, and we are His. We are His people, the sheep of his pasture. ⁴ Enter His gates with thanksgiving; go into His courts with praise. Give thanks to Him and praise His name. ⁵ For the Lord is good. His unfailing love continues forever, and His faithfulness continues to each generation.

O: Observations. Pray and ask God to show you things in the passage and in your key verse.
Who is being talked to?

_____

What is being said to them? (What commands are found in this passage? What warnings are given? What promises are made?)

_____

Where is this being said or written from and is that important to what you are reading?

_____

_____

Are there words that are emphasized and/or being used more than once? What are the definitions of important words?

_____

_____

Using a tool for cross-referencing, what do other verses in the Bible add to your understanding of this verse or passage?

_____

_____

Looking at commentaries or Study Bible notes, what do you learn about this passage?

How does what you learn help you understand and know God better?

A: Application. What does this mean to you? How does this apply to your life?

Is there a command you should obey? Is there something you should start or stop doing? Is there a promise you should claim as a believer in Christ?

P: Prayer. Write out or pray based on what you have learned and what the Lord wants to apply to your life. Ask God to move in your heart and fill you with His Spirit as you pray this. Pray for others that God is bringing to mind as you were studying this section of scripture.

DAY 3

S: Scripture. Romans 12:1-3 (NASB)

¹ Therefore I urge you, brothers and sisters, by the mercies of God, to present your bodies as a living and holy sacrifice, acceptable to God, which is your spiritual service of worship. ² And do not be conformed to this world, but be transformed by the renewing of your mind, so that you may prove what the will of God is, that which is good and acceptable and perfect. ³ For through the grace given to me I say to everyone among you not to think more highly of himself than he ought to think; but to think so as to have sound judgment, as God has allotted to each a measure of faith.

O: Observations. Pray and ask God to show you things in the passage and in your key verse.

Who is being talked to?

What is being said to them? (What commands are found in this passage? What warnings are given? What promises are made?)

Where is this being said or written from and is that important to what you are reading?

Are there words that are emphasized and/or being used more than once? What are the definitions of important words?

Using a tool for cross-referencing, what do other verses in the Bible add to your understanding of this verse or passage?

Looking at commentaries or Study Bible notes, what do you learn about this passage?

_____
_____
_____

How does what you learn help you understand and know God better?

_____
_____
_____

A: Application. What does this mean to you? How does this apply to your life?

_____
_____

Is there a command you should obey? Is there something you should start or stop doing? Is there a promise you should claim as a believer in Christ?

_____
_____

P: Prayer. Write out or pray based on what you have learned and what the Lord wants to apply to your life. Ask God to move in your heart and fill you with His Spirit as you pray this. Pray for others that God is bringing to mind as you were studying this section of scripture.

_____
_____
_____
_____
_____

DAY 4

S: Scripture. Colossians 2:7 (NLT)
⁷ Let your roots grow down into him, and let your lives be built on him. Then your faith will grow strong in the truth you were taught, and you will overflow with thankfulness.

O: Observations. Pray and ask God to show you things in the passage and in your key verse.
Who is being talked to?

_____

What is being said to them? (What commands are found in this passage? What warnings are given? What promises are made?)

_____

_____

Where is this being said or written from and is that important to what you are reading?

_____

_____

Are there words that are emphasized and/or being used more than once? What are the definitions of important words?

_____

_____

Using a tool for cross-referencing, what do other verses in the Bible add to your understanding of this verse or passage?

_____

_____

Looking at commentaries or Study Bible notes, what do you learn about this passage?

How does what you learn help you understand and know God better?

A: Application. What does this mean to you? How does this apply to your life?

Is there a command you should obey? Is there something you should start or stop doing? Is there a promise you should claim as a believer in Christ?

P: Prayer. Write out or pray based on what you have learned and what the Lord wants to apply to your life. Ask God to move in your heart and fill you with His Spirit as you pray this. Pray for others that God is bringing to mind as you were studying this section of scripture.

DAY 5

S: Scripture. Isaiah 29:13 (NLT)
¹³ And so the Lord says, "These people say they are mine. They honor me with their lips, but their hearts are far from me. And their worship of me is nothing but man-made rules learned by rote.

O: Observations. Pray and ask God to show you things in the passage and in your key verse.
Who is being talked to?

_____

What is being said to them? (What commands are found in this passage? What warnings are given? What promises are made?)

_____

_____

Where is this being said or written from and is that important to what you are reading?

_____

_____

Are there words that are emphasized and/or being used more than once? What are the definitions of important words?

_____

_____

Using a tool for cross-referencing, what do other verses in the Bible add to your understanding of this verse or passage?

_____

_____

Looking at commentaries or Study Bible notes, what do you learn about this passage?

_____
_____
_____

How does what you learn help you understand and know God better?

_____
_____
_____

A: Application. What does this mean to you? How does this apply to your life?

_____
_____

Is there a command you should obey? Is there something you should start or stop doing? Is there a promise you should claim as a believer in Christ?

_____
_____

P: Prayer. Write out or pray based on what you have learned and what the Lord wants to apply to your life. Ask God to move in your heart and fill you with His Spirit as you pray this. Pray for others that God is bringing to mind as you were studying this section of scripture.

_____
_____
_____
_____
_____
_____

DAY 6

S: Scripture. Psalm 95:1-6 (NLT)

¹ Come, let us sing to the Lord ! Let us shout joyfully to the Rock of our salvation. ² Let us come to him with thanksgiving. Let us sing psalms of praise to him. ³ For the Lord is a great God, a great King above all gods. ⁴ He holds in his hands the depths of the earth and the mightiest mountains. ⁵ The sea belongs to him, for he made it. His hands formed the dry land, too. ⁶ Come, let us worship and bow down. Let us kneel before the Lord our maker.

O: Observations. Pray and ask God to show you things in the passage and in your key verse.

Who is being talked to?

_____

What is being said to them? (What commands are found in this passage? What warnings are given? What promises are made?)

_____

_____

Where is this being said or written from and is that important to what you are reading?

_____

_____

Are there words that are emphasized and/or being used more than once? What are the definitions of important words?

_____

_____

Using a tool for cross-referencing, what do other verses in the Bible add to your understanding of this verse or passage?

_____

_____

Looking at commentaries or Study Bible notes, what do you learn about this passage?

How does what you learn help you understand and know God better?

A: Application. What does this mean to you? How does this apply to your life?

Is there a command you should obey? Is there something you should start or stop doing? Is there a promise you should claim as a believer in Christ?

P: Prayer. Write out or pray based on what you have learned and what the Lord wants to apply to your life. Ask God to move in your heart and fill you with His Spirit as you pray this. Pray for others that God is bringing to mind as you were studying this section of scripture.

DAY 7

S: Scripture. Hebrews 12:28 (NLT)
²⁸ Since we are receiving a Kingdom that is unshakable, let us be thankful and please God by worshiping Him with holy fear and awe.

O: Observations. Pray and ask God to show you things in the passage and in your key verse.
Who is being talked to?

What is being said to them? (What commands are found in this passage? What warnings are given? What promises are made?)

Where is this being said or written from and is that important to what you are reading?

Are there words that are emphasized and/or being used more than once? What are the definitions of important words?

Using a tool for cross-referencing, what do other verses in the Bible add to your understanding of this verse or passage?

Looking at commentaries or Study Bible notes, what do you learn about this passage?

How does what you learn help you understand and know God better?

_____
_____
_____

A: Application. What does this mean to you? How does this apply to your life?

_____
_____

Is there a command you should obey? Is there something you should start or stop doing? Is there a promise you should claim as a believer in Christ?

_____
_____

P: Prayer. Write out or pray based on what you have learned and what the Lord wants to apply to your life. Ask God to move in your heart and fill you with His Spirit as you pray this. Pray for others that God is bringing to mind as you were studying this section of scripture.

_____
_____
_____
_____
_____
_____
_____
_____

WEEK 6
Identity and Purpose

In order for you to really GROW as a Disciple, you need to discover and understand who God created you to be.

READ EPHESIANS 2:10 (NLT)

For we are God's masterpiece. He has created us anew in Christ Jesus, so we can do the good things He planned for us long ago.

God made you to be you and He made you to be amazing. There is not another "you!" Your brain has 100 trillion neurons that are unique and no one else has a brain that is like your brain! Your eyes are so unique that a retinal scan can distinguish you from billions of other people who are on the face of the earth. No one in all time has had your fingerprints. God has a unique plan for you that is only for you. God has given you a God-given identity and God has given you a God-given purpose. He did all of this because He loves you!

READ PSALM 139:14-18 (NLT)

¹⁴ Thank you for making me so wonderfully complex! Your workmanship is marvelous—how well I know it. ¹⁵ You watched me as I was being formed in utter seclusion, as I was woven together in the dark of the womb. ¹⁶ You saw me before I was born. Every day of my life was recorded in your book. Every moment was laid out before a single day had passed. ¹⁷ How precious are your thoughts about me, O God. They cannot be numbered! ¹⁸ I can't even count them; they outnumber the grains of sand! And when I wake up, you are still with me!

What does this Psalm tell you about how God made you?

_____

_____

What description does David, the Psalmist, state that applies to you?

_____

What does this passage tell you about the plan that God has for you and for your life?

_____

_____

John Burke in his book *Imagine Heaven* gives many accounts of people who had near-death experiences. These accounts are about people who died and were clinically dead, then they left their bodies and went to either heaven or hell.

It is intriguing and profound that Burke says the first person you will meet in heaven is you. Think about that, the first person you will meet in heaven is you!

God made you to be an amazing, incredible, unique you.
And what we are seeing today is that most people don't know who they are and what their God given identity is. With people not sure about who they are, they don't know what they are made for. As a result, there is an assault being waged where people's God-given identity is under attack and their God-given purpose is being distorted.

In the coming sections I want you to conduct a research project so that you can meet you. I want you to discover your identity and have a good idea of what God's purpose for you is so you can live it out. You also need to have a clear picture of your love language and how your family background has been used by God to make you, you.

John Burke in *Imagine Heaven* gives us an in-depth insight into why this is vital:
> "'Who defines who you are?' This is such a critical question, but so few of us have really stopped to answer it. Who has the right to define who you are? What you're worth? What your purpose is? Whether you succeed or fail? How you define your identity is ultra-important.

What you believe about yourself is what shapes all your decisions and actions. Most of us end up believing things about our identity that are not grounded in God's reality—who God created us to be, what God created us to do. We believe lies about our identity that the evils of this world inflict on us. We constantly worry about the opinions or approval of others. We experience intense anxiety when we're not succeeding or are not recognized for our accomplishments. We feel sick inside when the stock market drops, or we don't get promoted. We find ourselves lowering our standards to new levels, then justifying it in order to prove our worth or get someone to love us.We feel the need to control our spouse or our kids because our identity has somehow gotten wrapped up in what others think or do."

YOUR GOD-GIVEN PERSONALITY

I am always amazed how the personality you have is given to you by God. It is implanted within you. Our parents don't give us our personality. As a parent your job is to discover your child's unique personality.

There are two personality tools we are suggesting for you to use to discover your God-given personality. One is called the Myers Briggs Type Sorter and the other is the Enneagram. Both will give you insight into who you are and your unique personality.

Myers Briggs Type Sorter
This gives you one of sixteen possible personality types that best fits you. This test will help you discover what your inclinations are and why you make the choices you make. This will help you to be aware of what energizes you and what drains you.

Human Metrics is based on Carl Jung's and Isabel Briggs Myers' typological approach to personality. You can find the link to take the Test at **www.CrossroadsChurch.com/growjournal**

Now that you have taken the test, write down what your personality type is.

What are the main characteristics of your type?

_____

_____

What characteristics do you feel are most true and which ones are you not sure are you?

_____

_____

_____

What does it say your inclinations are? What are your strengths?

_____

_____

_____

What jobs are recommended for people with your personality type? What is the commonality that you see in these jobs? Do these jobs sound like something you would like? What insight does this give you into the "you" God created you to be?

_____

_____

_____

The Enneagram

The Enneagram is a popular personality test that is based on you being one of 9 personality types. Historically many believe this dates back to early Christian leaders coming up with an understanding of who people are based on one of the seven deadly sins (which becomes an inclination for you when you are not at your best).

You can find the Enneagram personality test options at
www.CrossroadsChurch.com/growjournal

What number are you on the Enneagram? What are the main descriptors of that number? What ones are true of you? What ones are you not sure are true of you?

___

What are your motivations or strengths? What are your objections or fears? What is your core weakness (deadly sin) that you need to be aware of?

___

What do these 2 assessments tell you about you?

___

Your Love Language

Gary Chapman opened our eyes to the fact that the God of Love has created different languages by which we experience love and express love.
There are five main love languages, and some resonate with you more than others. You need all five, but the question is, "What are your main love languages?" What love language is the one that God gave you as the way you experience love at the deepest level? Knowing this helps you understand the "you" God created you to be.

The Five Love Languages are...
1. Words of Affirmation
2. Acts of Service

3. Physical Touch
4. Gifts
5. Quality Time

Go to **www.CrossroadsChurch.com/growjournal** so that you can be directed to a test that will help you discover the love language(s) that most deeply reflect who you are.

What are your top two love languages?

_____
_____

What does this tell you about you?

_____
_____
_____

YOUR FAMILY BACKGROUND

Another aspect of your identity is your family background. Do you come from a good family or one that suffers from a degree of dysfunction? What good traits have you developed because of your family and what baggage are you carrying because of your family?

One thing to keep in mind is that while your family may have problems (and all families have problems to one degree or another) these problems do not have to define you or have power in your life.

Joseph had a horrible family. In Genesis chapters 37-50, we see the dysfunction in Joseph's family. His father showed him blatant favoritism and his brothers were incredibly jealous of him. His brothers were often lazy and tended to be dishonest. Then his brothers abused him, rejected him, and sold him into slavery!

Note what Joseph told them later in their lives:

READ GENESIS 50:20 (NLT)
You intended to harm me, but God intended it all for good. He brought me to this position so I could save the lives of many people.

Joseph ended up being one of the Pharoah's trusted advisers, having immense power and using it to save many people. What does this tell you about God being able to change the bad in your family and in your past to something good?

_____

_____

READ ISAIAH 51:1-2A (NLT)
¹ "Listen to me, all who hope for deliverance— all who seek the Lord! Consider the rock from which you were cut, the quarry from which you were mined. ² Yes, think about Abraham, your ancestor, and Sarah, who gave birth to your nation.

Here we are told that if we hope for deliverance from a corrupt world and all that comes against us that we need to look at the "rock from which you were cut." Then it says to look to your ancestors. The rock is your family and we need to look and see how our family, our ancestors and our family history has shaped who we are for the good and for the bad.

What is your family background? What kind of relationship did your parents have? What about others in your family, your grandparents, aunts, uncles, cousins?

_____

_____

Was your family loving? Was your family fun? Was your family close?

_____

_____

How were disagreements and conflicts handled in your family?

_____

_____

Did your family show you unconditional love or did you feel like you had to earn their approval?

_____

_____

What did you learn or get from your family, good and/or bad?

_____

_____

_____

Do you have any toxic cycles within your family spanning multiple generations? Maybe anger, lying, addictions, broken relationships, areas of physical and/or mental illnesses? These can be seen as generational curses. Abraham, a key figure in the Bible, had a generational curse of anger in his family, and we see his story in Genesis chapters 12-17.

_____

_____

_____

_____

Remember that Jesus can and will break the generational curse when we commit our lives and all that we are to Him. Look at what we are promised in the Bible:

2 CORINTHIANS 5:17 (NASB)
> Therefore if anyone is in Christ, he is a new creature; the old things passed away; behold, new things have come.

Are there some old things from your family or in your life that need to pass away and not be true of you or for you any longer?

_____

_____

Look over what you wrote about your family, what does this tell you about you?

_____
_____
_____

YOUR HEART'S DESIRE(S)

Another unique aspect that is a part of your God given identity is found when you know the desires of your heart. God gives you the desires of your heart and then get ready; God gives you the desires of your heart. In other words, God puts desires in your heart that make you, you and that are a huge part of your God-given purpose. When you are seeing the desires of your heart happening then you are filled with passion and joy. You are energized and you are living the abundant life that Jesus said He wants for you to live.

READ PSALM 37:3-6 (NASB)
3 Trust in the Lord and do good; Dwell in the land and cultivate faithfulness.
4 Delight yourself in the Lord; And He will give you the desires of your heart.
5 Commit your way to the Lord, Trust also in Him, and He will do it.
6 He will bring forth your righteousness as the light and your judgment as the noonday.

What are we told we are to do? What are we told God promises to do?

_____
_____

A Heart's desire could be for…
- Adventure
- Love
- Children
- To experience Nature
- To see the World
- To build an orphanage or hospital to help those in need
- To help those who are oppressed
- To help others find healthy relationships
- And more…

What are the desires of your heart?

Reflect on all that you have researched about yourself and your God-given purpose. What stands out to you?

How can you be more the "you" God made you to be? How can you start to do more of what God made you to do?

Conclusion

Crossroads has a God-given vision to be a Tree of Life in a world of death. God has called for us to do this by seeing every single person who is in the Crossroads family be a true disciple of Jesus. We do this because He loves us, and we love Him. When we do then we will be a Majestic Tree that does not stand alone, and we will go in the Way of Miracles. When we do, we will not just talk about being Christians, but we will live in the Power of God
(1 CORINTHIANS 4:20).

So, get ready for what God has for you and for us. Get ready to see these promises be your reality!

1 CORINTHIANS 2:9-10 (NLT)
⁹ That is what the Scriptures mean when they say, "No eye has seen, no ear has heard, and no mind has imagined what God has prepared for those who love him." ¹⁰ But it was to us that God revealed these things by his Spirit. For his Spirit searches out everything and shows us God's deep secrets.

PSALM 1:1-3 (NASB)
¹ How blessed is the man who does not walk in the counsel of the wicked,
Nor stand in the path of sinners,
Nor sit in the seat of scoffers!
² But his delight is in the law of the Lord,
And in His law he meditates day and night.
³ He will be like a tree firmly planted by streams of water,
Which yields its fruit in its season And its leaf does not wither;
And in whatever he does, he prospers.

EPHESIANS 3:20 (NLT)
Now all glory to God, who is able, through his mighty power at work within us, to accomplish infinitely more than we might ask or think.

JEREMIAH 33:3 (NLT)
Ask me and I will tell you remarkable secrets you do not know about things to come.

Made in the USA
Coppell, TX
10 November 2022